OVERCOMING AN

imperfect

BOSS

A Practical Guide to Building
a Better Relationship With Your Boss

KARIN HURT

Printed in the United States of America

ISBN-13: 978-0615977256
ISBN-10: 0615977251

BOOK DESIGN CARRIE RALSTON, SIMPLE GIRL DESIGN LLC

FOR MARCUS, WHO SEES MY IMPERFECTIONS
AND LOVES ME ANYWAY.

AND BEN AND SEBASTIAN, TWO LEADERS GROWING
IN THE EXUBERANT CHALLENGE OF IMPERFECTION.

**MAN WAS MADE AT THE END OF THE WEEK'S WORK,
WHEN GOD WAS TIRED.**

— MARK TWAIN

TABLE OF
contents

FOREWORD

Dr. Henry P. Sims, Jr.

Karin's deliberate choice of the word "boss" in her title is more than a bit ironic. I believe she may even hate the implications of the B word more than I do.

As I wrote in *Business Without Bosses*, when we use the word "boss," we typically mean an individual who influences subordinate employees through such leader behaviors as command, instruction and top-down goal assignments, frequently accompanied by a healthy dose of reprimand and intimidation — a "Do it my way or else!" approach.

Bosses can generate compliance, especially in the short-term. They have a tendency to create "yes persons" who are willing to comply but lack initiative and creativity.

With a boss, the locus of innovation is always top-down. Subordinate employees seldom venture forth with their own creative ideas. Their mental powers are centered on trying to say and do as the boss wishes.

Instead, we need SuperLeaders: leaders who lead others to lead themselves.

I've watched Karin grow as a SuperLeader for over two decades. Even as an executive, she's never been a "boss." In fact, I've enjoyed her stories of the many "bosses" and other managers up, down and sideways whom she's influenced to become stronger, empowering leaders.

Karin's long track record of breakthrough results as an executive in sales, customer service, marketing, and human resources proves that SuperLeadership is worth fighting for, even when it means persuading your bosses to let you lead in style that scares them.

The practical advice Karin shares in *Overcoming an Imperfect Boss* is a must-read for leaders yearning to make a deeper impact with their career. This book will help you to become the boss you wish you had.

Dr. Henry P. Sims, Jr.
Professor Emeritus, University of Maryland

Coauthor of eight books, including: *Business Without Bosses*, *Company of Heroes*, *The New SuperLeadership* and *Share, Don't Take the Lead*.

INTRODUCTION

I keep being asked why, of all the leadership topics I write and speak about, I would pick "imperfect bosses" as the topic of my first book. It's quite simple: the supervisor relationship is the number one predictor of employee engagement and job satisfaction. Yet, most people screw up this powerful association.

The tragedy is that too many people leave the magic of what could be a game-changing relationship untapped. They follow traditional boss-subordinate protocol…they don't get too close, don't say too much, and don't push the envelope. And so bosses come and go, and both parties muddle through. People do their best with the boss they've been given.

It doesn't have to be that way.

Some of the bosses who once made me crazy grew to be lifelong mentors and friends. As I reflect on our journeys, each of these alliances had a transformation point. Something drove one or the other of us crazy, we talked about it, worked through it, and emerged with a deeper level of respect for one another

IMPERFECT BOSSES I HAVE KNOWN

There was the Vice President that blew a gasket because of a stupid (yet fixable) mistake one of my employees had made. He screamed and yelled at me just minutes before I had to grab a microphone and give a motivational speech to my entire organization.

I had choices. I could have become rattled and let his poor leadership choice screw up my ability to lead. Instead, I looked him in the eye and calmly shared, "I can see you're really upset, and I'm sorry. We need to talk through what happened here and address it. But right now, I have hundreds of people waiting for inspiration. So please excuse me." I turned around and left my office, not sure if I would have a job when I returned.

I gave my speech, fixed the mistake, and his entire demeanor changed. We never did discuss that outburst or what had triggered it. We didn't need to. This "screamer" never raised his voice to me again, and became one of the best bosses and mentors I've ever had.

There was also the time I was running a large sales organization. I knew we needed to change the organizational structure and invest in additional headcount. I had a tight business case, and had proved out the trial concept, but my boss was worried about the political ramifications of doing something different than the other regions.

I told him, "I'm so confident that this will work that if it doesn't, you can fire me." Of course, that was highly risky, and I had to be prepared to walk away. But the depth of my passion and commitment led him to "yes."

We blew away the results, and became the best sales team in the nation in that arena. Others regions followed our model.

THE IMPERFECT BOSS I HAVE BEEN

Of course, sometimes I'm the imperfect one in need of reigning in.

Not long ago, I was going through a really tough couple of weeks. The cocktail of challenges was impacting our performance. We needed stronger results immediately. I didn't realize how much my stress showed on the outside until a trusted leader on my team shared bluntly, "You're changing."

The words stung with fierce truth. He was right. Succumbing to the leadership squash sandwich, I was taking on familiar but unwelcome behaviors common in such scenes. I was showing up like the boss I'd refused to become.

I was worried about our mission, our cause, and our careers. My passion to protect my team had taken on an ironic intensity. My supportive style had morphed into frantic control. I began inviting myself to calls and requiring more rehearsals and executive readouts. Instead of trusting my competent team, I scrutinized each page of every PowerPoint deck.

My efforts to protect them from my stress had backfired.

I had stopped leading like me.

The words still echoing from the first conversation, my phone rang again. I now knew my team was tag-teaming this intervention.

"I joined this organization because I believe in your leadership. Your rare style works. Stay the course. We believe in you, in us, and the mission. Every one of us has your back. Just tell us what you need."

There I was, a leader following the intervention of my team. They were coaching me back toward authenticity and it was wonderful.

My team reminded me that...

- Showing up tough is weak
- Servant leaders must also receive
- Great teams hold their leader accountable
- I want to know the truth
- Great leaders tell the truth
- Courage means staying true to your style
- My team needs me to lead like me

Over the years, I've had employees tell me how I've hurt their feelings, overlooked their efforts, embarrassed them, or over-reacted. Every one of those conversations has made us stronger, tighter, and more effective.

The most brave of these folks, the men and women who have given me the most stinging (and true) criticism, have grown into the closest of friends.

THE IMPERFECT BOSS YOU HAVE

I know some of you are saying, "That may work well and good for you, but you've never met anyone quite like my boss, the big jerk." Well, it's possible, but not likely. I've known my share of Looney Tunes over the years. We'll talk about that scene too.

This book is designed to empower you to tackle the most difficult situations with your boss, and to give you the courage and the techniques to invest more deeply in your relationship. Use the ideas and tools to help your boss become the boss you need, and to help you become the boss you wish you had.

Overcoming an Imperfect Boss is designed as an interactive working guide. Review the scenarios and jot down your ideas, complete the exercises, and share the survey with your boss.

If you're also a boss, share the book with your team and have them help you.

If you've got tough scenes I've not covered here, drop me a line at karin.hurt@letsgrowleaders.com and let's think them through together.

CHAPTER 1

great expectations

One of my favorite bosses had such highs and lows that we gave her two nearly matching Barbie dolls for her desk. The first was immaculately dressed in typical Barbie fashion, matching shirt, shoes and pearls. The other doll wore ripped clothes, had magic marker on her face, and hair that looked like it had been eaten by a cat.

We chose a "good Barbie day" to approach her with our plan. Our request was that she put the doll out that best portrayed her mood as a warning sign. We knew if "evil" Barbie was lurking, we needed to lay low. Not ideal for sure. No one wants a moody boss.

And yet, she accepted the gift with a smile. She used the dolls, as requested, for our benefit. Thankfully, she got the point when one of us went to her shelf and switched the dolls.

She was a Customer Service VP who took a big chance on me, a pregnant HR Director who had never worked in a call center or led a large team. She offered me a customer service executive position, despite the fact that I would have to go out on maternity leave in the middle of my learning curve. Her immediate peer thought she was nuts.

She helped me learn, while giving me the freedom to lead. She tapped into my HR background and let me lead bigger projects that leveraged my skills. She threw a great baby shower, and hand-knitted a baby blue blanket for my son.

We both grew deeply in that relationship, and dramatically improved the business. With all that, I could accept a bit of grouchy from time to time.

I'm sure you have similar stories…

> *"She had great vision, but I never knew exactly what she was thinking."*

> *"I learned more that year than any time in my career, but he never supported me in a promotion."*

> *"He really let me run my own show, but I doubt he knows what I really accomplished."*

> *"He pushed me to take important risks, but he never got to know me personally."*

> *"The work was exciting and fun, but she didn't respect any boundaries to create work-life balance."*

Take a moment to consider your favorite boss…

- What were his or her greatest strengths?
- What drove you crazy?
- What did you learn in working with his or her imperfections?
- How did you emerge stronger as a result?

The perfect boss is as elusive as the ideal mate. And yet, we're frustrated when our leaders fall short of our impossible expectations.

We long for leaders who will...

- Engage us in a compelling vision
- Have the utmost integrity
- Be authentic and transparent
- Treat us kindly and fairly
- Develop, mentor, and coach us
- Empower and trust us
- Communicate clearly
- Motivate us
- Be competent and knowledgeable
- Have a sense of humor

Bosses who think they're great, are the most frightening. It's usually the strongest leaders who have the lowest tolerance for their bosses' bungles.

Strong leaders think, "I'd never treat MY team THAT way…which PROVES he's a jerk."

The truth is, he's just an imperfect human doing the best he can. Just like you.

WHY IT'S HARD

The boss-subordinate relationship is unnatural by design. We sell our power for money. We look to a person we have not chosen (whom we may or may not respect) for affirmation, evaluation, and reward.

In order to "succeed," we strive to figure out what will make this guy like us, and adjust our style accordingly. We take every criticism to heart, even when we don't believe it.

We take this already unnatural structure and impose even more awkward performance feedback systems.

Imagine if we burdened our home relationships with some of the same formal systems we impose at work.

"Honey, I've decided to give you an end-of-year appraisal. Your cooking's improved and you're taking out the trash without being reminded, you get an A in housework. But you've been so stressed lately; I have to give romance a B-."

We wouldn't even consider that stunt with our kids, where we have more power.

If such tactics wouldn't work with people who know and love us, why would we imagine they would enhance trust at work?

And so I offer these stories and wisdom based on years of being an imperfect boss and learning from the many imperfect bosses I've had the pleasure to know.

CHAPTER 2

the biggest mistake

The secret to a healthy boss-subordinate relationship is to remember that it's just that, a relationship. You're two messy human beings doing the best you can.

Beginning in the space of imperfection offers much freedom and power. It's not your boss's responsibility to motivate you, develop you, or direct your career. That's your job. Sure, the best leaders will help you grow, but never forget who's really in charge.

So if your boss doesn't have it to give, don't waste time being frustrated. Stop coveting thy co-worker's boss, and find the support you need.

Seeing your boss as a flawed human being has other benefits too. Instead of judging her on how well he's doing, focus on how you can best support him. Not in a "kissing up" or an "if I do this, he'll owe me that" sort of way. But because you're two human beings in a relationship, working on the work.

Regardless of whether your boss is the best one ever, or a royal pain in the tuckus, there's a good chance your boss also...

- Wants you to succeed
- Is dealing with pressures you don't fully understand
- Sometimes feels overwhelmed
- Is trying to please a boss, too

- Is working to balance work and family
- Is doing the best he or she can
- Could use your help

There's the age-old adage: Always make your boss look good. I find it also useful to make them feel good — reduce their stress by making their jobs a bit easier.

WAYS TO SUPPORT YOUR BOSS

If you haven't asked your boss the obvious question, "How can I best support you?", do that today.

Some bosses will be great and give you a list. Most will likely give you a vague response or tell you you're doing just "fine." So, here are a few fail-proof tips for supporting your boss.

SWEAT THE SMALL STUFF

Do what you say you will do, without needing to be reminded. Get ahead of deadlines. Administrative stuff is a drag; your boss has better things to do than to chase down your paperwork.

COMMUNICATE FREQUENTLY IN BULLETED SUMMARIES

Leaders often suffer from information overload. They are often called upon to summarize complex issues on the fly; that's not when they want to go digging through emails to find the details they need. Resist the urge to cc and forward emails without a summary attached.

UNCOVER ISSUES AND ADDRESS THEM

Your boss knows there are problems and shielding her from them will only make her nervous. Lift up the issues you find, along with solutions to address them. She will sleep better knowing you are paying attention and are all over it.

THANK HER FOR HER HELP

Be honest and specific. Done well (and privately) this is not brown-nosing — it's feedback that can help her help you. A side benefit... she will grow as a leader.

DOCUMENT YOUR ACCOMPLISHMENTS

It's not bragging — it's useful. Well-timed, detailed summaries help to support the performance management process.

CHAPTER 3

tough scenes

With all this imperfection going on, you'll need a leg up on the tough situations.

In this chapter, I offer ten tough scenes to inspire your thinking, along with some tips for approaching such situations.

To make the most of this book, read the scenario then jot down your strategy. Then, read the additional tips. There are no right answers. In fact, I'd love to hear what you come up with.

Drop me a line with your thoughts or additional scenarios at karin.hurt@ letsgrowleaders.com

Scene 1

How Do I Get My Boss to Trust Me?

Cooper loves his boss, Jackie. She treats him as her go-to guy and has been told he's "ready now" for a promotion. But when he gets to work on Tuesday, he finds Jackie is moving to Tampa in a new assignment. John is taking over her role. The rest of the team's a bit worried, but not Cooper. He knows Jackie's put in a good word with John.

After the initial "honeymoon" phase, John starts digging in to learn the new gig. He questions Cooper's thought processes and wants more detail behind decisions. He asks for formal readouts each week and invites himself to meetings Cooper normally ran himself. Cooper's frustrated and hurt with the extra oversight.

What should Cooper do?

Take a minute to jot down your ideas...

Advice for Cooper

It's natural for Cooper to be frustrated. After all, he's still the same guy doing the same work. But frustration can easily make matters worse. Acting entitled to trust will raise more suspicion.

Developing trust takes time, and it starts over with each new relationship. Sure a reputation of results helps, but it's still about building a personal connection.

Cooper should ask John what he needs most as he transitions to his new role. Being available and supportive will go a long way. He should resist the urge to talk about his own needs (or career) at first. Sure that's important, but he should wait until John's feeling more comfortable in his role. Beyond that, he should stay the course with his high-integrity, results-focused approach to the work. Let the great work speak for itself. The trust will follow.

TIPS FOR GETTING YOUR BOSS TO TRUST YOU

DO WHAT YOU SAY YOU WILL DO

Keep your commitments — every time. Integrity and consistency are vital to trust. If you have to change your commitment, communicate quickly and explain why.

FOLLOW THROUGH

This one is slightly different from the first tip. Follow through involves looking at the outcomes of your actions and ensuring they achieved the desired result. "Doing what you say" is not enough if it did not produce the right outcome. There is more work to do. Do it, or ask for help.

DEVELOP GREAT PEER RELATIONSHIPS

Your boss cares what other people are saying about you. She wants to know you work well with others, offering and asking for help when needed.

FOLLOW THE "NO BLIND SIDE" RULE

This is the one I see break down the most. Always be the first to share your own bad news and what you are doing about it. Don't let your boss get wind of a breakdown through the grapevine (or worse, from their boss).

KNOW THE DETAILS

Your boss will trust you when you know what you are doing. She will be less likely to want to know every detail if she is sure that you do.

ASK WHAT ELSE YOU CAN DO TO HELP

No boss wants to wonder if their people have enough to do. If you have extra bandwidth, offer to do more. Your boss will then trust that you have plenty to do when you are not asking.

Scene 2

How Do I Persuade My Boss?

Kathy's convinced her boss, Carl, is making a bad decision. She gets the financial pressure he's under, but if she can't secure the funding, the project will be in jeopardy. All attempts to persuade him have failed. Kathy's worried her continued pushing will damage her career. She's tempted to give in. After all, he's the boss.

But, deep in her heart she knows she's right. She cares. It matters. Others are counting on her.

What should Kathy do?

Take a minute to jot down your ideas...

Advice for Kathy

Of course, every boss is different. Kathy must understand and play to Carl's style. Most importantly, she must keep her cool and take it offline. These conversations are best done one-on-one. No one wants to be challenged in front of a group. She should start by asking questions, and really ensure she understands the whole picture. There may be a lot more going on than she understands.

Kathy should do her homework with lots of supporting data and facts. She would also do well to stakeholder her ideas with other folks Carl trusts, and ask them to support her argument.

TIPS FOR PERSUADING YOUR BOSS
(THE P.E.R.S.U.A.D.E. MODEL)

Don't just jump into these conversations. A calm, well-planned approach will help convince your boss to do the right thing.

Private

Whatever you do, don't confront him in front of your peers, his peers, your team...you get the picture. Take it offline.

Emotion

Let your passion inspire your argument, but don't emote. Stay calm. Appeal to his heart and mind, but don't wear your heart on your sleeve. It might help to tell a story, but think it through first. Overly emotional appeals will weaken your argument.

Research

Do your homework. Prepare for questions. Do the math. Do more math. Do the math his way. Poke holes. If he doesn't like math, collect stories. Do more math, just in case.

Share

Share your concern frankly. Speak your truth. Share why you are concerned for the business. Have several supporting points.

understand

Listen **carefully**. He's got broader perspective and more contexts. Learn as much as you can. Hear him out completely and suspend judgment. Listen some more.

Acknowledge

Appreciate his point of view. He's likely not a jerk. He's got pressures too. Understand them. Learn all you can. Consider…deeply.

Data

If you're still convinced of your position, enrich your data. Build graphs. Show correlations. Draw pictures. Find stories. Benchmark with the best.

Engage

Engage your supporting team. For me, this usually means the finance gal…she's fantastic…yours can be too. In my last gig it was the finance guy. These folks are more reasonable than you think. Convince others to care about your point of view. Get a light murmur of whispers started to support your cause in their own words.

scene 3

How Do I Give My Boss Bad News?

Mike trusted his team to complete the project on time. They didn't check all the facts, and they overlooked a key concern. The delay will be at least a week. He's furious, but the worst part is, he knows he has to tell Shelly, his boss. In fact, Shelly will want to tell her boss too.

It's time for Mike to come clean.

How does Mike tell Shelly the bad news?

Take a minute to jot down your ideas...

Advice for Mike

The good news…if Mike handles this well, it could increase his leadership credibility. The bad news…he's still got bad news. Mike should stay calm and take accountability for the situation. It's vital that he not blame the team or others. As he explains the situation, he should present a solution, along with other alternatives he explored.

TIPS FOR GIVING YOUR BOSS BAD NEWS (THE D.A.R.N. METHOD)

The biggest mistake to make when giving bad news is waiting too long. Your boss would rather know what's going on, even if you don't need her help. Use the D.A.R.N. method to guide your approach.

Disclosure

(EXPLAIN THE SITUATION AND ROOT CAUSE)

"I've had a bad day. We have a bit of a situation, and I need to fill you in. _____ happened…and now we have_____ . When I dug in deeper I learned it was caused by _____ (behavior or situation not person)."

Accountability

(DON'T BE A BLAMER)

"I accept full responsibility. I should have been closer to this. Here's how I can prevent a similar outcome. _____ ."

Response
(SHARE YOUR SOLUTION)

"Here's what I've already done _____ (it's important to have something to say here)."

Next Steps
(SHARE YOUR PLAN AND WHAT YOU NEED)

"Here's what I'm going to do next_____ . I could use your help with _____ (if needed)."

Scene 4

What If My Boss Is Disengaged?

Justin works hard and has always gotten along with his boss. But his new boss, Carol, is driving him crazy. She just doesn't seem to care. She passed empowering a long time ago, and is now just missing. He asks Carol for feedback, and she says everything is "fine." His updates fall into a black hole. He's worried about his team, and his career.

What should Justin do?

Take a minute to jot down your ideas…

Advice for Justin

Justin should start by talking with Carol about how he can best support her, as well as what he needs. If she's really checked out, he needs to proactively find other ways to meet his needs.

Justin should seek out mentors and other advocates. Also, peer relationships become even more important. This is a great time for him to step up into additional leadership responsibility and bring forth his new ideas.

It's important he works to package and market his team's work with other key stakeholders.

BENEFITS OF WORKING FOR A DISENGAGED BOSS

Ideally, your boss is interested, eager to remove roadblocks, asking provocative questions, and helping build your career. That's the leader I wish for you, and want you to be. But, with 71% of workers disengaged, chances are one day or another you'll work for a disengaged boss.

Cheer up; played well, there's upside to a disengaged boss.

FREEDOM TO EXPERIMENT

Don't go crazy, but try creative approaches to improve the business. Pilot that new idea. Try leading differently. Enjoy the freedom to try new things without the need to constantly read out on your every move. Then package your success stories and share best practices.

BROADENED NETWORK

Your boss is not the only one you can learn from. Having a disengaged boss can push you to broaden your network. Seek out mentors and other advocates. Look for opportunities to interface with his boss. Invest in your peer relationships.

MARKETING YOUR WORK

You're going to have to work a bit harder to get your work noticed. Use this opportunity to build those skills. Work on streamlining your emails and improving your presentation skills. Schedule time with your boss and others to share information and get the feedback you need. Reach out to other stakeholders.

STRATEGIC THINKING

A disengaged boss will force you to work a level up. Consider what you would say in his position. Learn as much as you can about the bigger context for your work. Be the boss you wish you had.

TEAM BUILDING

Nothing brings teams together more than a common cause. Invest deeply in your peers. Leverage one another's skills. Support each other's development. A disengaged boss won't be around for long, but your peer relationships can last through your whole career.

Scene 5

What If My Boss Is Moody?

Laura loves her boss, Gretchen — sometimes. The problem is, she never knows which boss she's going to get. Sometimes she's awesome, but other times she feels like she can't do anything right. She's afraid any conversation on the subject would backfire. Lately, she's just found herself avoiding her.

What should Laura do?

Take a minute to jot down your ideas...

Advice for Laura

Maybe it's a side effect of passion, intensity, or commitment, but some of the most interesting bosses I've had have a moody dark side. Moody at any level is tough to be around. If it's your boss, it's even trickier. It's tempting to avoid the mood (and the person who wears it) and just try to survive. But if you can take the Emotional Intelligence (EQ) high road, you may find a rich relationship waiting to be forged just below that annoying surface.

TIPS FOR DEALING WITH MOODY BOSSES

FIND A SAFE WAY TO TALK ABOUT IT

Find a safe way to raise the topic. It's tempting to address the mood during the mood, because that's when your emotions are high as well. Pick a calmer time to talk about, or bring in humor, as in the first chapter.

NOTICE THE PATTERNS

You wouldn't force your kids to eat peas right after they woke up from a nap. If you're dealing with a moody boss, notice the patterns and, whenever possible, choose your timing. Chart the outbursts and see if there's a discernable pattern. Learn the triggers and the timing. (And don't screw this up by leaving the chart on your desk.) ;-)

UNDERSTAND ROOT CAUSE

When someone accuses you of being moody, your likely reaction is probably, "Well, I may be a bit tired, or hormonal, or stressed...BUT...the issue is real." Moody bosses feel that way too. Reduce their crankiness by addressing the underlying causes.

DON'T REWARD THE BEHAVIOR

Don't coddle. If you succumb to hysterics, the tantrums will continue. Stay calm and suggest another time to discuss the issue. Your boss may be angry if you walk away, but once he cools off, he will likely appreciate your approach.

KEEP YOUR COOL

Bad moods are contagious, so immunize as much as possible. Recognize the behavior for what it is, and don't take it personally. If it's really not about you, then let yourself believe that. Of course, this takes us back to the third tip...be sure you understand your part in the moodiness mix master.

Scene 6

What If I'm Asked to Represent My Boss?

Jenny sits in on conference calls for her boss all the time, but this meeting is different. Her boss, Bruce, asked her to represent the team at the big meeting in headquarters while he's on vacation in Disneyworld with his family.

She knows this is a great opportunity to get noticed by some key executives, but she's nervous. How can she be sure she represents Bruce, the work, the team, and herself well?

What should Jenny do?

Take a minute to jot down your ideas...

Advice for Jenny

Jenny should get as many insights as possible about the people attending the meeting, and the way they typically roll. She should over-prepare. It's likely she knows more about some aspects of the project than others, so she should be sure she can represent the work her peers are doing in the best light.

If the topic is controversial, she can stakeholder her ideas offline with one or two key players in advance and ask for their support. Most importantly, Jenny should not be afraid to speak up and share her views. Folks will be watching how she leverages this important opportunity.

TIPS FOR REPRESENTING YOUR BOSS WELL

UNDERSTAND THE NORMS

However silly it may seem, there is likely an established protocol for getting work done. Don't be a distraction by going against the flow. Fitting in will make even your more radical ideas more palatable.

Approach the scene like kids playing jump rope on a playground. Watch the rope spin a few times before jumping in. How does the communication flow? Is there a seating arrangement? Don't let a silly mishap leave you looking like a rookie.

DO YOUR HOMEWORK

Knowledge inspires confidence (in you and from them). Carefully review agendas in advance. Talk to your peers and get up to speed on familiar topics. Prepare beyond expectations. Learn what you must to lead effectively in this context.

STAKEHOLDER YOUR BIG IDEAS

If you're just sitting in for a meeting, talk to your boss about using this as an opportunity to bring up that new idea. If it's a longer-term gig (such as an acting assignment), you'll have a window to showcase even more capabilities. Take time to stakeholder your ideas offline with key opinion leaders. Ask them to help you fine-tune your thinking and presentation. You will feel more confident, and the idea will "sell" better with a few key supporters.

SPEAK UP

Leaders often waste their seat at the table. Sure, they take good notes and report back, but they must also seek to influence. You have great insights — share your truth. Resist the urge to just nod in agreement.

BUILD DEEPER RELATIONSHIPS

However temporary, a seat at the table is a great way to build deep connections. Build relationships and professional intimacy with your temporary peers. Let them know who you are and what you value. Be extraordinarily helpful.

Scene 7

Why Doesn't My Boss See My Potential?

Tom thinks he's ready to be promoted. His boss, Alex, doesn't. Alex has known Tom for years, and to him, he'll always be "Tommy." Sure, the familiarity is nice, and he's always great to his kids, but Tom has grown in ways that Alex can't seem to see.

What should Tom do?

Take a minute to jot down your ideas…

Advice for Tom

Tom should start by thanking Alex for all the support over the years, and share specifics about how he's used his advice to grow. He should also ask for straight talk with specifics about areas he still needs to develop. He could also ask for specific development opportunities, like shadowing Alex or attending some meetings on his behalf.

TIPS FOR CONVINCING YOUR BOSS YOU'RE READY

UNDERSTAND HIS PERSPECTIVE

Work to truly understand his view. It's likely that your current performance is a factor. Understand what you're doing well in your current job from his perspective, as well as where things are breaking down. Resist the urge to talk about "promises" made by other leaders, or your expectations based on those discussions.

BE REAL

Share what you're feeling and why. Gently share specific examples if it feels right. Laugh about how you're just not "Tommy" anymore. He'll relate…he was once a "Tommy" to someone, too.

SHADOWING

Ask if you can hang out with him for a day or two. Be sure to emphasize you want the "real deal." If there's a late-night fire drill, you want to be included. Ensure you understand what the next level is really all about.

SKIP LEVEL MEETING

Ask if you can have a skip level meeting with his boss for development. Ask for feedback on perceptions and what you can do to be most ready to support the company's objectives.

STORIES

Share your career story. Be open about your disappointments. Help him take the long view of how you've grown.

DEVELOPMENT PLANS

Listen carefully to the feedback and suggest a few developmental options to grow in these arenas. Ask for other specific ideas to include. Be sure to place time frames around them and follow up upon completion.

Scene 8

I Don't Know Where I Stand

Every time Elizabeth asks her boss Carol for feedback, Carol tells here she's "doing great." But this is Elizabeth's fifth year in the same job and she's starting to wonder. She's watched peers who don't seem any more qualified get promoted or selected for special assignments. Her performance reviews are always solid, but never outstanding.

She likes her job and the people she works with, but she's beginning to feel like she's treading water. Her mentor tells her, "Just ask your boss," but every time Elizabeth tried to approach the subject, she chickened out.

What should Elizabeth do?

Take a minute to jot down your thoughts…

Advice for Elizabeth

Elizabeth needs to set up a meeting with her boss only on this topic, rather than trying to squeeze it in as a footnote to some other meeting. She should also do it outside the context of a formal performance review.

Elizabeth should start by telling her boss how interested she is in insights. She should express her desire for deeper feedback that will help her improve. She must listen carefully, ask clarifying questions as needed, but be sure not to argue back.

She doesn't have to agree with it all, but she wants to keep the door open for richer insights.

QUESTIONS YOU SHOULD ASK YOUR BOSS

- What specifically can I do to better support our team's mission?
- What do your peers say about me?
- If your boss were to give me one piece of advice, what would it be?
- Who should I be working with more closely?
- What could I be doing to make your job easier?
- To what do you attribute your own career success? How can I be more effective in that arena?
- Which parts of my style concern you the most?
- Specifically, what do I need to work on to be ready for (insert the job or assignment you are most interested in here) _____ ?

QUESTIONS YOUR BOSS MAY ASK YOU

One of the best bosses I've ever had mentors hundreds of people in our company. He is a very busy Senior Vice President, but he'll meet with anyone...however, first they have to answer his 43 questions. He finds this intimidating enough that it weeds out casual employees looking for a quick fix and leads to richer conversations with those who take the process seriously. He sent me his updated list recently to share. Here are a few of the gems...

- What are the things that excite and energize you about your work here?
- What are the things that drain or frustrate you about your work here?
- What have you done to reduce this frustration?

- If you were a superhero, what powers would you have? How would your powers help our company?

- How is your work/family balance? If not satisfied, what are you doing to change it for the better?

- How many people on your networking list would leave their position (or company) to join your leadership in a new department or company?

- What is your "sound?" How are you perceived by others; eg, a Harley Davidson has a unique sound that differentiates itself from other motorcycles. What is your business? How would others describe you? Would they know this the first time you met?

- What are some of your outside interests? What are the skills you are leveraging in these outside interests?

- What is your marketing or sales approach?

- We are at your retirement celebration. What position do you hold that you are retiring from at this time?

Scene 9

My Boss Is Fine, But His Boss Scares Me Out of My Socks

Maia was visibly shaken as she left the readout with her boss's boss — let's just call her "Meany." Maia's results are solid, and she was prepared to share her team's story. She just hadn't anticipated Meany's line of questioning. She could feel the conversation going south, and then she choked. The questions turned to sarcasm mixed with a few "Gotcha's."

What should Maia do?

Take a minute to jot down your ideas…

Advice for Maia

Maia should breathe and do anything else in her power to keep her cool. If she's really lost control, a quick break may be in order. She should also try to determine where the meeting broke down. Was she overly optimistic? Did she not give enough details? She should do what she can to address those gaps. Executives like to give their opinion. Whatever she does, she should tell the truth about what she knows, and commit to follow-ups on anything she doesn't know.

It's also a good time to ask some questions and make the meeting interactive.

Most importantly, Maia needs to realize that the big freeze happens to everyone from time to time. She can't let that shake her confidence. She should look for opportunities to get back in front of the executives again soon.

TIPS FOR COMMUNICATING WITH EXECUTIVES

PREPARATION

The most important way to prepare for an executive meeting is to ask yourself these questions:

- What key message do you want me to remember?
- What do you need me to do?
- Why should I believe in you?

Write them down. Know these so well that no matter how nervous you get, they serve as the foundation for anything else that will come out of your mouth.

OTHER PREPARATION TIPS

- Anticipate the questions based on executives in attendance (i.e., Finance, HR, Field)
- Understand every number and point on the slides
- Have back-up data
- Understand your back-up data (sounds obvious but can be trickier than you think)
- Ensure your boss is aligned with everything you are going to share (never blindside your boss)

ENSURE YOUR SLIDES ARE ROCK SOLID

- Less is more; keep the slides clean and simple
- Avoid cutesy graphics and distracting movement
- Include trending
- Forecast improvement; "Based on this plan, I commit to having this metric be at (x) by (date)."

TIPS FOR YOUR TALK TRACK

- Begin with a problem statement, then share actions
- Call out the opportunity first; if something is a problem point it out (before your audience does)
- Ask for what you need
- Be brief and be gone (don't keep asking for more questions, quit while you're ahead)
- Acknowledge and thank your peers (in the room and outside of it)
- Reference previous presentations ("As Jane just shared…")
- If you don't know an answer…DON'T make one up
- Resist the urge to share how hard you worked

5 BIG MISTAKES WHEN COMMUNICATING WITH EXECUTIVES

1. OVERCONFIDENCE

Executives are suspicious of rose-colored glasses. Even if you're passionate about your results, water down your exuberant optimism with an equal dose of concern. If it's going great, speak to "early positive indicators" or about being "cautiously optimistic." Throw in a few things you're worried about for good measure. Executives like to worry — throw them a bone.

2. LACK OF CONFIDENCE

Don't send executives to bed at night worrying if you're the right guy for the job. Show up strong and knowledgeable. Listen to questions carefully and share your expertise. Balance accomplishments with plans to resolve your biggest concerns.

3. OVER-DISCLOSURE

Tell the truth elegantly, and then shut up. You know a lot; avoid the temptation to prove it. You don't want those executives getting involved in minutia. Unless you're a big fan of more readouts and escalations, share what's relevant and move on.

4. FORGETTING TO BREATHE

The tendency to spew will undermine your credibility. I've been in more than one executive review where the speaker was instructed to "take a breath." Pause for questions. Make it a conversation.

5. IGNORING THE ASK

Even if they don't ask — ask for what you need — executives want to contribute, but aren't sure where to jump in. They'll feel better, and you'll get what you need.

THE SECRET

The secret to executive communication is credibility. Work on building trust and connection in every interaction. Trusted advisors build a track record of solid decisions and successful projects. Layer on appropriate confidence and carefully crafted words, and your project and relationship will prosper.

Scene 10

My Boss Likes Me, But My Peers Think I'm a Kiss Up

Ryan's driven, ambitious, and successful. His boss, Jerry, loves him and has put him on the fast track. His peers are getting snarky, but Ryan's never worried too much about that "crap." "They're just jealous…."

But Jerry's starting to notice the tension, and he's told Ryan to work on his "peer relationships" as part of his development plan. Ryan has no idea where to start.

What should Ryan do?

Take a minute to jot down your ideas…

Advice for Ryan

Peers impact your performance more than your boss. Your boss is one person. Your peers are an army of potential support, with diverse skills and talent. They've got resources and best practices that can save vital time. They're facing similar challenges. Some of them are working together with beautiful synergy.

Ryan needs to open up to his peers and tell them he's working on improving his relationships. He should ask how he can be most helpful, and about what behaviors are getting in the way. Sincere one-on-one conversations will go a long way. He should consider the following list of behaviors that may be ticking off his peers.

5 REASONS YOU'RE TICKING OFF YOUR PEERS

1. NEVER ASK FOR HELP

You're not cocky, just busy. You know they're busy too. But your lack of reaching out is easily viewed as arrogance. You're sending signs you're "too busy," so your peers don't bother.

Ask for advice now and then. Be sure to really listen to the response. When you do get help, publicly express your gratitude. If you doubt they have much to offer, I can't help you. Prepare for an extra dose of snarky.

2. CHALLENGE THEM IN FRONT OF THE BOSS

Your peer feels belittled and bruised as he climbs from under the bus you didn't even know you were driving. You didn't mean to be a jerk, it's just you weren't paying attention until now. The first time you expressed your concerns was in front of the boss (or worse yet, the boss and others). The boss agrees and once again praises your quick thinking. *Peer feedback is best given off-line. Give your input early, and then you can nod in full support of the enhanced plan.*

3. WITHHOLD BEST PRACTICES

You're trying some wild and crazy ideas, and you don't want to share before you know they'll work. Or you got busy and forgot to share. I know you'd never purposely withhold your great ideas, but your peers may not have the same interpretation. *Let folks know what you're up to. If it's half-baked, describe the batter and promise updates. Peers trust peers who share what they're doing.*

4. TAKE THE CREDIT

When the praise is coming your way, it's easy to get caught up in the emotion. *At your level you did not do this alone. Pause, consider, and deflect the praise. Your peers will appreciate the gesture, and all will respect your* **confident humility**.

5. REACT POORLY TO FEEDBACK

The surest way to lose friends and alienate people is to reject their feedback. If you stop hearing, they'll stop talking (well, at least to your face). *Be gracious and open to what they have to say. Pause to consider. If it's stupid,* **shake it off**. *But always take the high road and thank them for their input.*

CHAPTER 4

when a good boss
relationship goes too far

L ike other good things in life, a tight boss relationship, taken to extremes, can wreak havoc with your career. I've seen otherwise smart and talented people lose credibility by over-aligning with a boss. Be sure to diversify your relationship investments.

Perhaps you'll recognize these characters. Avoid these common traps.

THE COATTAIL RIDER

On the surface it feels like the perfect symbiotic relationship. You're her right-hand guy. You work hard and always achieve results. She gets promoted to a new department, and she brings you over. It's comforting for her to have someone familiar she can rely on, and you get a promotion, or a new assignment. Win-win, right? Then it happens again, and again. Sweet deal?

Although it's comfortable and feels like the fast track, beware of riding coattails, particularly into more than one assignment. Your identity will become enveloped within your more powerful boss. People will begin to see you as a package deal. If her career derails, so will yours.

Also, the best leadership growth comes from working with a variety of leaders. Although the devil you know feels easy, you're both limited in the growth you would get from working with a wider variety of leaders. Better to let your relationship morph into a mentoring relationship, or friendship, while you each continue to pursue the next steps of your careers.

THE MINI-ME

Your boss is successful, so you work to emulate his every move. You begin dressing more like him and picking up his mannerisms. After all, it works for him, why not for you? In fact, you may not even notice you're doing it. Trust me, others do.

No matter how great a leader your boss is, resist the urge to lead like him. Your best leadership will come when you lead from a place of deep authenticity. No one wants to follow a copycat.

THE TAG-ALONG

Your boss is looking to develop you, and has your best interest at heart, so he brings you along...a lot: to the big meetings, to the charity fundraiser, to happy hour. When there's a company function, there you are right by his side. You always find your way to his table at dinner.

After all, powerful people hang out with other powerful people, right? Be careful. Some such exposure is healthy but overexposure will burn. Give your peers a chance for face time. Be deliberate in getting to know other people at those functions. It's harder, sure, but the widened network will be invaluable.

THE NAME-DROPPER

When you're trying to get stuff done, it's tempting to just throw around your boss's name. "Karin said this MUST be done by tomorrow at 5." Weak leaders hide behind the power of other leaders. Even if your boss is the one asking for something to be done, resist the urge to use that muscle. In the long run, you'll have much more credibility when you own your asks.

THE GOOD SOLDIER

Your boss says jump, you say how high…every time. Now, of course, there's a time and a place for good soldiering, but real leaders know when to question and put on the brakes. Sure, your boss may reward you for your consistent execution of her directives, but she'll be amazed when you challenge her with innovation and suggest creative and better alternatives.

Work to build a fantastic relationship with your boss, but beware of such co-dependencies. What feels easy and comfortable could damage your career.

CHAPTER 5

what if he's really a jerk?

Now, you may be thinking, "Seriously, I wish, my biggest problem was that I'm too close to my boss. My boss gives new meaning for the word jerk." Read on.

If you think your boss is a jerk, and everyone else does too, I challenge you to go deeper. Get to know her. Tell her the truth. If everybody's frustrated, she knows it. Chances are, under all that crap, she is starving for help. Don't bring the band…or the wagon. Someone will speak the truth, why not you?

DON'T LET A BAD BOSS MAKE YOU A JERK

Whatever you do, don't sit around commiserating about the jerk. Stay focused on the work and avoid the gossip. If you need to talk to someone, choose HR or other formal support.

Pay close attention to how the stress is impacting you, your team, and your family. Find folks who will tell you the truth. Jerky behaviors are contagious, so be sure you're staying true to your leadership philosophy.

Find ways to ground yourself: exercise, meditation, and prayer are all good options. Remember that you are you, and this jerky boss is just one transient person in your life. This season will end, but you will live with who you are becoming forever.

USE THE EXPERIENCE TO DEVELOP YOUR LEADERSHIP

You can learn as much from a bad boss as a good one. Pay close attention to the impact your boss's behaviors have on you and your teammates. What doesn't kill you will make you a stronger leader. Keep a journal or make a running list. Make a vow to never be "that guy."

"MAYBE I SHOULD JUST QUIT"

"People don't quit jobs, they quit people." If you're a leader, know this is true. If people keep leaving for "other opportunities," it's not them, it's you.

But if you're considering leaving your job because of a boss, think well. Bosses come and go. Don't waste all you've invested because of one jerky guy.

On the other hand, if your jerky boss is just one part of the problem, look deeper. Your boss may be reacting to your behavior or your impact on the team.

Consider other indications you may be in the wrong job.

9 INDICATIONS YOU'RE IN THE WRONG JOB

1. GROUCHY

If you're grouchy all the time, it's likely bigger than a boss problem. Notice the patterns and which parts of the job suck away your life force.

2. NOT MAKING AN IMPACT

When your effort exceeds your results, you're likely to feel defeated. Setbacks are natural. But if you're giving your all, and you just can't win, you may be in the wrong role.

3. UNABLE TO FIND "YOUR PEOPLE"

If you've got no kindred spirits in sight, that's a sign. If you can't find any leaders you respect to mentor you, or learn from, begin networking outside your company and see who shows up.

4. NOT USING YOUR SKILLS

No job will use all your gifts, but if your job uses none of them, something's wrong.

5. EMOTIONALLY EXHAUSTED

If even the fun stuff feels hard, it might be time for a change. If there's no energy left for the afterwork activities that make life good, that's an even bigger indicator.

6. TRAPPED

If all your motivations come from the periphery, not the job — money, benefits, fear of having failed — it's time to look around. You secretly wish you'd get fired, find a new job, before you do.

7. OVERWHELMED

If it's gone from invigorating and challenging to, "It's all too much. There's no way to get it all done," it may be time to go.

8. QUIET

If you refuse to talk about work to your family or friends, that's not good. Your work is a big part of your life — you should want to share. If the question, "How was your day?" makes your hair curl, it's time to get a new job (or a flat iron).

9. SICK

If you're getting sick more than usual, and a day off makes it worse, consider the pattern. If you get a "Sunday night headache" every Sunday thinking of returning to work, it's time to assess why.

BEFORE YOU QUIT...

It may be you're in the wrong job. That's okay. There's a right job out there. Quitting doesn't make you a quitter.

Some suggestions:

Go slow. It's much easier to get a job when you have a job.

Keep up the effort at your current job. Don't quit in place.

Take care of yourself. Take a vacation. Take time to exercise and sleep.

Think about other jobs (or volunteer gigs) that you loved. What skills did you use? What did you find most fulfilling? Make a list of these characteristics.

Arrange for informational interviews. Learn more about jobs you may enjoy.

TALK TO YOUR BOSS (PAUSE FIRST)

Share your feelings and explore options. Your boss may be relieved that you see the issue. Listen. There may be ways to modify your situation, or find other jobs within the organization that are a better fit.

CHAPTER 6

be the boss you wish
you had: an exercise

The glorious side effect of having an imperfect boss is it makes you think. Notice what you value most in your boss and what drives you crazy.

On the following page is an exercise that will help.

STEP 1: CONSIDER YOUR IDEAL BOSS

What would your ideal boss….value, do, think, say? Take a few minutes to write this down in the quadrants. Give your ideal boss a name (i.e., dynamic Diane or Caring Connie) and put it in the center square.

DESCRIBE YOUR IDEAL BOSS

VALUE	DO
THINK	SAY

STEP 2: CONSIDER YOUR OWN STRENGTHS AND CHALLENGES

Now complete a similar exercise based on you...your own strengths and challenges. Give yourself a name. For what do you want to be most known?

For a bonus round, give the matrix to your team and get their thoughts.

DESCRIBE YOUR LEADERSHIP

VALUE	DO
THINK	SAY

STEP 3: COMPARE THE GRIDS

How are you most like and unlike the boss you wish you had?

STEP 4: IDENTIFY WHAT'S HELPING AND HURTING YOUR LEADERSHIP SUCCESS

What negative forces prevent you being the leader you most want to be? Politics? Stress? Write them down.

Negative Forces:

-
-
-
-
-

Positive Forces:

-
-
-
-
-

STEP 5: IDENTIFY SPECIFIC ACTIONS

Identify three specific actions you will take to become more like your "ideal" boss. Write them down here.

Action _____

By When _____

Who to Involve _____

Who Can Help _____

Action _____

By When _____

Who to Involve _____

Who Can Help _____

Action _____

By When _____

Who to Involve _____

Who Can Help _____

CHAPTER 7

holding a real conversation

The best way to have a healthy boss relationship is to keep the conversation open. As with all human relationships, it's useful to check in from time to time. Earlier in this book, I offered questions as conversation starters.

Some may find it useful to have a more formalized way to open the conversation, and so I offer this easy REAL relationship assessment. Pick a window once or twice a year for you to each complete this assessment independently, and set up some quiet time to discuss.

I don't recommend using this at the same time as your formal mid-year or end-of-year appraisals. Emotions are generally higher during those times. This conversation deserves its own meeting at a separate time.

MANAGER/EMPLOYEE SELF-ASSESSMENT

Please take a few minutes to assess your relationship on each component of the REAL relationships model. The manager and employee should each complete independently, and then use as a springboard for dialogue.

REAL RELATIONSHIPS

MANAGER/EMPLOYEE SELF-ASSESSMENT

REAL FOCUS AREAS	STRONGLY AGREE	AGREE	NOT SURE	DISAGREE	STRONGLY DISAGREE
RESULTS					
Our work together leads to breakthrough results					
I feel supported by you in overcoming mistakes and setbacks					
You are committed to helping me achieve my professional and career goals					
RESULTS TOTAL					
ENERGY					
You help me tap into my gifts and strengths					
I'm energized by our interactions					
You support my healthy work-life balance and need for rest and renewal					
ENERGY TOTAL					

REAL RELATIONSHIPS

MANAGER/EMPLOYEE SELF-ASSESSMENT

REAL FOCUS AREAS	STRONGLY AGREE	AGREE	NOT SURE	DISAGREE	STRONGLY DISAGREE
AUTHENTICITY					
You do what you say you will do					
I trust you to tell me the truth					
I feel comfortable being myself around you					
AUTHENTICITY TOTAL					
LEARNING					
You provide me regular feedback to help me improve					
You support me in my development					
You challenge me to improve					
LEARNING TOTAL					
OVERALL TOTAL					

4 SIGNS OF A R.E.A.L. BOSS RELATIONSHIP

Results

You've got great results. Sure, there are a lot of factors that influence results, but having a great relationship with your manager helps. If you really like the guy, but you're not winning, your relationship may be snuggly, but may need some fine-tuning to be truly effective. Although great results are the end-game, how you handle mistakes matters as well. Great boss relationships survive and even thrive after well-intentioned screw-ups.

Energy

Working together is exciting and fun. You recognize and leverage each of your unique gifts. You find ways to tap into peripheral skills that light you up. You look forward to your interactions. When the work gets really stressful, you support one another versus adding to the pain. You both recognize the need for rest and renewal and support a healthy integrated life.

Authenticity

You can count on one another to tell the truth and to follow-through on commitments. You aren't afraid to be yourself and you invest in getting to know each other as people. You share how you're really thinking and feeling, and can count on one another to keep confidences.

Learning

You're constantly challenging one another to improve. You proactively offer feedback and recognize success. You feel stretched, yet scaffolded in your risks. You support each other on your quest for continuous improvement. Learning together feels healthy and fun.

AFTERWORD
a challenge

Leadership is never handled...not for your boss, or for you. Consider your relationship with your boss a learning laboratory.

Leverage every interaction with your boss to improve your own leadership. Be the boss you wish you had.

If you lead other leaders now, open up this conversation with your team. Have them identify their ideal boss, and learn what you could do better. Use these vital, messy human relationships to work on your leadership while you work on the work.

Grow leaders who'll become the boss you'd want. Be the boss they need you to become.

ACKNOWLEDGEMENTS

This is the hardest part of the book to write. I've been surrounded by so much love and support in my growth as a leader and writer. If I've overlooked you, know you are in my heart.

Thank you, God. My leadership and writing is a highly spiritual practice. Thank you for your patience.

My love and gratitude go to Marcus, my husband and intimate partner in this amazing life journey. To my sons, Ben and Sebastian, who light up the world with their positive energy. To my parents, Jean and Larry, who inspired leadership in all three of their children — through sacrifice, involvement, examples, and quiet lessons of what matters most.

I'd also like to thank the Let's Grow Leaders community. I'm humbled and overwhelmed with the interaction and support in every blog post. Your insights are woven throughout this book.

To the wonderful international leadership writing community — and to all the contributors to the Let's Grow Leaders Frontline Festival, thank you for thought leadership and friendship.

An extra shout-out to Dan Rockwell whose guidance and support has been invaluable from my first few months of blogging. To Lolly Daskal, whose beautiful friendship inspires me on many levels. To Mike Henry Sr., and all the folks doing great work to lead change. To Becky Robinson, who has supported me from the early days and is growing with me.

A big thanks to LaRae Quy, Terri Klass, Alli Polin, and Chery Gegleman with whom I've spent many a long night collaborating on our next book on Energizing Leadership.

Thank you,Carrie Ralston, for your creativity and beautiful design work.

I must also thank all the imperfect bosses I have learned from over the years. I've received deep gifts from each of you — far too many to name. A few who have a special place in my heart: Gary Creighton (who fought with me to change the "system" — rest in peace — I'm still "on it"; Ray Wierzbicki (who shares my passion for skipping to work); Maureen Davis (who gets it), and Gail Parsons, Chris Baron, and Tami Erwin (who invest deeply). And a special thanks goes to my mentor of over two decades, Dr. Henry Sims (the ultimate SuperLeader). Oh, and an ironic fist bump of gratitude to the one or two jerks I've worked with over the years…for helping me understand the extreme cost of bad leadership.

And finally, to the thousands of amazing human beings I've had the honor to lead over the years. Thank you for your deep investments in our missions and yourselves. Together, we've accomplished more than I could have ever imagined. I only hope you've learned something from all my imperfection. I'd be remiss not to give a special shout-out to Wayne Smith and Jonathan Green, my co-conspirators in a building leadership oasis. And to my current team, who know that at any minute, their name will be disguised and they'll appear in a blog post. Thanks for growing with me.

Namaste.